THE UNEXPLAINED

THE
MUMMY'S
CURSE

BY JEREMY WESTPHAL

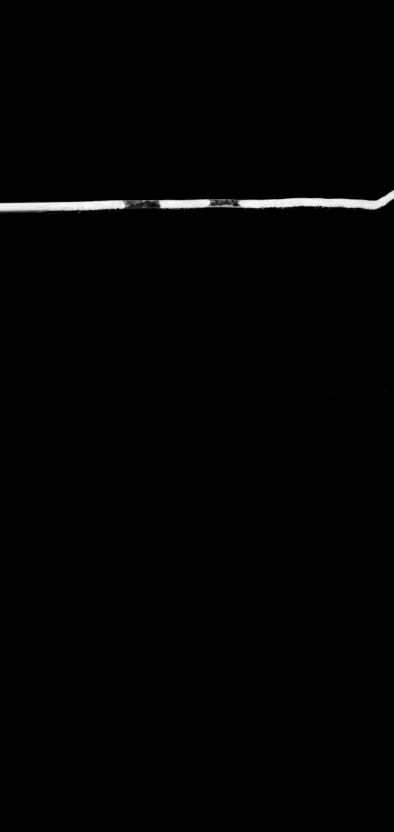

BELLWETHER MEDIA · MINNEAPOLIS, MN

Are you ready to take it to the extreme?
Torque books thrust you into the action-packed world
of sports, vehicles, mystery, and adventure. These books
may include dirt, smoke, fire, and dangerous stunts.
WARNING: read at your own risk.

Library of Congress Cataloging-in-Publication Data

Westphal, Jeremy.
 The mummy's curse / by Jeremy Westphal.
     p. cm. -- (Torque: the unexplained)
 Summary: "Engaging images accompany information about the Mummy's Curse. The combination of
high-interest subject matter and light text is intended for students in grades 3 through 7"--Provided by
publisher.
 Includes bibliographical references and index.
 ISBN 978-1-60014-643-5 (hardcover : alk. paper)
 1. Tutankhamen, King of Egypt--Tomb--Juvenile literature. 2. Blessing and cursing--Egypt--Juvenile
literature. I. Title.
 DT87.5.W47 2012
 932'.014--dc22   2011002254

This edition first published in 2012 by Bellwether Media, Inc.

Printed in the United States of America, North Mankato, MN.

CONTENTS

CHAPTER 1
AN ANCIENT CURSE?

In November of 1922, **archaeologist** Howard Carter made a great discovery in Egypt. Carter found the **tomb** of a famous Egyptian **pharaoh** named Tutankhamun. It was located in an area called the Valley of the Kings. The tomb held King Tut's **mummy** and many riches. The find made news around the world.

Egypt

Valley of
the Kings

However, strange things began to happen after the discovery. A cobra ate Carter's pet bird the next day. The man who paid for the dig, Lord Carnarvon, died just weeks after he visited the tomb. He had a mosquito bite that became infected. Others who explored the tomb also suffered horrible fates over the next few years.

Lord Carnarvon

Ancient Egyptians thought cobras were the protectors of pharaohs in life and in death.

Rumors spread that the tomb was **cursed**. Some people thought **ancient** magic was at work. They believed it punished any person who dared to enter the tomb. Newspapers printed stories about the Mummy's Curse. Was the curse real?

KING TUT

Tutankhamun was only 9 years old when he became pharaoh. However, he died when he was 19. The cause of his death is unknown.

CHAPTER 2

WHAT IS THE MUMMY'S CURSE?

ncient Egyptians believed that the human **soul** lived beyond death. They built large tombs for their mummified pharaohs. They filled the tombs with riches. These items would be needed in the **afterlife**. Then the tombs were sealed tightly. The mummies were not to be disturbed.

Some people think the ancient Egyptians placed a curse on anyone who entered a tomb. Others believe that an Egyptian god is responsible for the curse. Anubis was the god of the dead and guard of Egypt's tombs. People say the curse is his revenge for anyone who enters a tomb.

The curse of King Tut's tomb is the most famous example of the Mummy's Curse. Some people believe that other tombs are also cursed. A few tombs have curses written on their walls in **hieroglyphics**.

ANCIENT WARNING

A message that warned about the Mummy's Curse was carved in a statue of Anubis. It read: "It is I who hinder the sand from choking the secret chamber. I am for the protection of the deceased."

Anubis

VICTIMS OF THE CURSE?

Many think these people fell victim to the Mummy's Curse after King Tut's tomb was opened.

Name

Lord Carnarvon

George Jay Gould

Aubrey Herbert

Hugh Evelyn-White

Sir Bruce Ingham

Georges Bénédite

Richard Bethell

Description

Lord Carnarvon paid for Carter's dig. He died several weeks after the discovery of the tomb.

Gould got a fever and died months after a visit to King Tut's tomb.

Herbert was Lord Carnarvon's half brother. He died of blood poisoning.

Evelyn-White helped Carter dig out the tomb. He hanged himself the following year.

Ingham was given an artifact from King Tut's tomb. Then his house burned down. He rebuilt it, but it washed away in a flood.

Bénédite died of heat stroke shortly after visiting the tomb.

Bethell was Carter's secretary. He was the second person to enter the tomb. He died of respiratory failure at the age of 35.

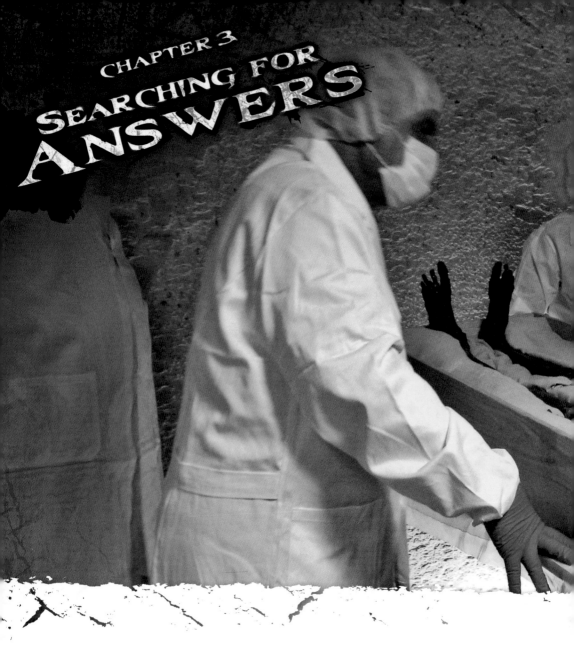

M any people believe that King Tut's tomb is a clear example of the Mummy's Curse. Others think the deaths and tragedies are unrelated to the opening of the tomb. People have come up with other **theories** about what happened.

Scientists have studied Egyptian mummies
and found types of **mold** that can make people sick.
The mold may have grown there by itself. The ancient
Egyptians could also have put it there.

Skeptics argue that the curse is not real. They point out that Howard Carter lived for 17 years after he opened the tomb. He spent many of those years in the tomb itself. How did Carter escape the curse if it was real? Carter wasn't the only survivor. Many people present when the tomb was opened were still alive several years later.

A FALSE WARNING

A newspaper reported that hieroglyphics on King Tut's tomb read: "They who enter this sacred tomb shall swift be visited by wings of death." It was a lie, however. The newspaper made it up to spread the idea of a curse.

Was the Mummy's Curse ancient magic? Was it the result of some strain of deadly mold? Or was it nothing more than a scary story? No proof of the curse has ever been found. Still, people tread carefully in the Valley of the Kings.

GLOSSARY

afterlife—spiritual existence after death

ancient—existing over 1,500 years ago

archaeologist—a scientist who studies ancient civilizations

cursed—affected by an evil spell that brings harm

hieroglyphics—an ancient form of writing that uses pictures to represent words and ideas

mold—a type of fungus that often grows in damp places

mummy—a dead body that has been preserved with oils and other substances for burial

pharaoh—an Egyptian king

skeptics—people who do not believe in something

soul—the spirit of a person; some people believe a person's soul lives on after he or she dies.

theories—ideas that try to explain why something exists or happens

tomb—a place where a dead body is buried

To Learn More

AT THE LIBRARY

Axelrod-Contrada, Joan. *The Kids' Guide to Mummies.* Mankato, Minn.: Capstone Press, 2011.

Harkins, Susan Sales, and William H. Harkins. *King Tut.* Hockessin, Del.: Mitchell Lane Publishers, 2009.

Lace, William W. *The Curse of King Tut.* San Diego, Calif.: ReferencePoint Press, 2007.

ON THE WEB

Learning more about the Mummy's Curse is as easy as 1, 2, 3.

1. Go to www.factsurfer.com.

2. Enter "Mummy's Curse" into the search box.

3. Click the "Surf" button and you will see a list of related Web sites.

With factsurfer.com, finding more information is just a click away.

INDEX

The images in this book are reproduced through the courtesy of: Rachelle Burnside, front cover; Getty Images, p. 4; Juan Martinez, p. 5; David Cole/Alamy, p. 6 (small); Dallas and John Heaton/Photolibrary, pp. 6-7; Kenneth Garrett/National Geographic/Getty Images, pp. 8-9; Herbert M. Herget/The Bridgeman Art Library/Getty Images, pp. 10-11; Ancient Art & Architecture Collection Ltd/Alamy, pp. 12-13; Lukiyanova Natalia, pp. 14-15; Barry Iverson/AP Images, pp. 16-17; Time & Life Pictures/Getty Images, p. 18; Hulton Archive/Getty Images, p. 19; Jon Eppard, pp. 20-21.